IS-914: Surveillance Awarness: What You Can Do

By

Fema

10/31/2013

IS-914 – Surveillance Awareness: What You Can Do

Course Welcome

The purpose of this course is to make critical infrastructure employees and service providers aware of actions they can take to detect and report suspicious activities associated with adversarial surveillance.

To achieve this goal, the course provides an overview of surveillance activities and the indicators associated with them as well as the actions that employees and service providers can take to report potential surveillance incidents.

Course Objectives

At the end of this course, you should be able to:

- Identify potential targets of adversarial surveillance.

- Describe the information obtained by surveillance that is of interest to adversaries.

- Recognize indicators of surveillance within the everyday environment.

- Identify actions that you can take to detect potential adversarial surveillance incidents.

- Describe the importance of identifying and reporting suspicious activities associated with adversarial surveillance.

- Specify actions you can take to report potential incidents of adversarial surveillance.

What is Adversarial Surveillance?

This course focuses on adversarial surveillance, which is conducted to gather critical information about individuals, organizations, businesses, and infrastructure in order to commit an act of terrorism or other crime.

Adversarial surveillance does not include activities conducted by security, investigative, law enforcement, or other personnel in the normal course of their duties, nor does it include taking photographs, recording video, or taking notes for other innocent purposes, such as photographing family and friends or documenting travel.

Taking Action Against Surveillance

This narrative presents an example that is based on a true story and demonstrates the importance of reporting suspicious surveillance when you observe it.

An employee on the way to work one morning noticed a vehicle with two passengers parked in an unauthorized area at the facility. As the employee passed by the car, the passengers asked for directions to another building nearby. But, when they left the parking lot, they proceeded in a different direction.

A couple of weeks later, the employee saw the same vehicle, once again parked in the unauthorized area. The driver sped away, but the employee took down the license plate information and reported both incidents to security, including a description of the original passengers.

Three weeks later, a different employee observed a person videotaping the same building in an unusual manner and reported the incident. Security personnel used the building's closed-circuit video to identify the person.

The person in the video was a match to the driver of the vehicle previously reported, and, when brought in to view the video, the employee from the previous incidents identified the videographer as the same person from before.

The security manager provided this information to law enforcement, resulting in an investigation. One of the individuals identified during the investigation was linked to a known terrorist money-laundering operation.

Because each of these separate incidents was reported, the incidents were able to be linked together as indicators of a potential terrorist attack.

Do you know what you should do if you see signs of adversarial surveillance?

Adversarial surveillance is conducted to gather information about individuals, organizations, businesses, and infrastructure in order to commit an act of terrorism or other crime.

This course will provide you with the information you need to detect adversarial surveillance and to report it.

Simple actions, such as taking this course and reporting surveillance activities when you see them, will help protect our Nation, our communities, and our workplaces.

Surveillance Detection: Three Simple Actions

This course will cover three simple actions you can take to help prevent terrorism and criminal surveillance activities.

1. **Understanding Surveillance**

    o   Identify the targets of adversarial surveillance.

    o   Recognize the purpose of adversarial surveillance.

    o   Know what information is collected during surveillance.

2. **Detecting Surveillance**

    o   Look for unusual behavior or activities.

    o   Recognize the indicators of adversarial surveillance.

3. **Reporting Surveillance**

    o   Determine (in advance) procedures for reporting incidents:

        ▪   Within your organization.

        ▪   To local law enforcement.

    o   Report suspicious activities using predetermined procedures and forms.

What Is Surveillance?

The word surveillance comes from the French word for "watching over."

Surveillance involves monitoring persons or locations to identify behaviors, activities, and other changing information.

Adversarial surveillance is distinguished by its purpose - to gather information in preparation for an action that is aggressive or criminal in nature. These actions include domestic and international terrorism, crimes against individuals, espionage, theft, stalking, and destruction of property.

Targets of Surveillance

Critical infrastructure assets and systems, as well as the people who frequent those locations, often are the primary targets of adversarial surveillance.

Examples include: places where large numbers of people gather such as stadiums and shopping malls; power and communications systems; food and water supplies; transportation networks; and financial entities and networks.

Emergency and law enforcement responders also frequently become secondary targets as they respond to an incident of terrorism.

Surveillance Targets

Terrorists historically have focused their attention on the following targets:

- Mass gathering points; any place where large numbers of people gather.

- National icons.

- Political and economic targets, such as government and financial centers.

Critical infrastructure assets and systems also often are the primary targets of adversarial surveillance by terrorists or other criminals.

The information below identifies why each critical infrastructure sector might be a target of surveillance in preparation for a terrorist attack.

Banking and Finance

The Banking and Finance Sector accounts for more than 8 percent of the U.S. annual gross domestic product and is the backbone for the world economy. As direct attacks and public statements by terrorist organizations demonstrate, this sector is a high-value and symbolic target.

Chemical

The Chemical Sector is an integral component of the U.S. economy, converting various raw materials into diverse products, many of which are critical to the health and well-being of the Nation's citizenry, security, and economy. Due to its size and the inherent dangers of many chemicals, the Chemical Sector may be an attractive target for attack.

Commercial Facilities

The Commercial Facilities Sector is represented by a wide range of assets, including, but not limited to, hotels, commercial office buildings, convention centers, stadiums, theme parks, residential buildings, shopping centers, and other sites where large numbers of people gather to pursue business activities, conduct personal commercial transactions, or enjoy recreational pastimes. The sector is a dominant influence on the Nation's economy. The majority of facilities in the Commercial Facilities Sector operate under the principle of "open public access," meaning that the public may move freely through these facilities without the deterrent of highly visible security barriers. The large numbers of people gathered together and ease of access make commercial facilities attractive targets for attack.

Communications

Communications are an integral part of the Nation's health and safety, economy, and public confidence. Our Nation's economic and national security relies on the security of the assets and operations of critical communications infrastructure. Past terrorist attacks and catastrophic natural disasters have emphasized the need to protect this critical infrastructure to ensure that the full range of preparedness activities can take place.

Critical Manufacturing

The Critical Manufacturing Sector is an integral component of the U.S. economy, contributing greatly to the U.S. gross domestic product and employing roughly 1 million of our Nation's workers. While the contributions the Critical Manufacturing Sector makes to the Nation are immense, they do not come without risk—the economic and strategic value of the industry may make it an attractive target for terrorists.

Dams

The Dams Sector is a vital and beneficial part of the Nation's infrastructure and continuously provides a wide range of economic, environmental, and social benefits, including hydroelectric power, river navigation, water supply, wildlife habitat, waste management, flood control, and recreation. The potential risks in the event of asset failures, regardless of causation, within the Dams Sector are considerable and could result in significant destruction, including loss of life, massive property damage, and severe long-term consequences.

Defense Industrial Base

The Defense Industrial Base Sector consists of government and private-sector organizations that can support military operations directly; perform R&D; design, manufacture, and integrate systems; and maintain depots and service military weapon systems, subsystems, components, subcomponents, or parts— all of which are intended to satisfy U.S. military national defense requirements.

Emergency Services

The Emergency Services Sector is a primary "protector" for other critical infrastructure sectors. The loss or incapacitation of Emergency Services Sector capabilities would notably impact the Nation's security, public safety, and morale.

Energy

A healthy energy infrastructure is one of the defining characteristics of a modern global economy. Any prolonged interruption of the supply of basic energy—electricity, petroleum, or natural gas—would do considerable harm to the U.S. economy and the American people.

Food and Agriculture

Interference with the food or agricultural infrastructure could have a devastating impact on the Nation's public health and economy. Securing this sector presents unique challenges because food and agriculture systems in the United States are extensive, open, interconnected, and diverse, and they have complex structures. Food products move rapidly in commerce to consumers, but the time required for detection and identification of attacks and contaminations, such as animal or plant disease introduction or food contamination, can be lengthy and complex. Therefore, attacks and contaminations on the Food and Agriculture Sector could result in severe animal, plant, public health, and economic consequences.

Government Facilities/National Monuments and Icons

Government facilities, and elements associated with them, represent attractive targets for terrorist groups and criminals because they:

- Provide unique services;

- Often perform sensitive functions; and

- Have significant symbolic value.

Because government facilities often are located inside privately-held buildings, those facilities become targets as well.

National monuments and icons memorialize or represent significant aspects of our Nation's heritage, tradition, or values. Many of these sites represent the foundation of the country, making them symbolic targets.

Healthcare and Public Health

The Healthcare and Public Health Sector constitutes a significant portion of the U.S. economy. Due to the diffuse nature of the sector, there are many targets for potential attack that are exceptionally hard to protect. Ensuring a resilient healthcare and public health system capable of withstanding disruption and poised to protect lives and health during emergencies is vital for the Nation's safety and security.

Information Technology

The Information Technology Sector is central to our Nation's security, economy, public health, and safety. Information technology systems enable the Nation's economic activity, which is essential to maintaining homeland and national security. Many other critical infrastructure sectors rely on the Information Technology Sector for products and services, including the reliable operation of networks and systems, and the movement and storage of critical data.

Nuclear Reactors, Materials, and Waste

Nuclear power plants are among the best defended and physically hardened critical infrastructure in the country. A terrorist attack involving a nuclear reactor, materials, or waste would be a significant security event regardless of the scope, especially if it resulted in release of radioactive material to the environment.

Transportation Systems/Postal and Shipping

The Nation's transportation, postal, and shipping networks involve an expansive, open, and accessible set of interconnected systems of airways, roads, tracks, terminals, and conveyances that provide services essential to our way of life. The sheer size and capacity of the sector, which moves, distributes, and delivers billions of passengers and millions of tons of goods each year, makes it a highly attractive target for terrorists.

Water

Drinking water is central to the life of an individual and of society. A drinking water contamination incident or the denial of drinking water services would have far-reaching public health, economic, environmental, and psychological impacts across the Nation. Other critical services such as fire protection, healthcare, and heating and cooling processes would also be disrupted by the interruption or cessation of drinking water service, resulting in significant consequences to the national or regional economies.

New York City Video Surveillance

The narrative sequences shown below were recorded by Dhiren Barot in April 2001 in New York City and were seized, along with detailed notes concerning possible targets, from an al-Qaida computer in Pakistan.

Dhiren Barot, an al-Qaida operative, visited New York City in April 2001 and conducted extensive surveillance of various financial targets, such as the New York Stock Exchange, the International Monetary Fund headquarters, and the World Bank, among other targets.

Barot's footage included scenes of the World Trade Center towers. While filming, he turned the camera on its side to simulate the buildings falling over, and Barot or an unseen man mimicked the sound of an explosion.

Despite the eerily foretelling nature of the video, Barot is not believed to have had prior knowledge of the 9/11 attacks.

Dhiren Barot was sentenced to life in prison after pleading guilty to conspiracy to murder in October 2006.

Surveillance and Targeting

When planning illegal activities – including terrorist attacks or other crimes – perpetrators may conduct surveillance to try to learn all they can about:

- The location.

- Building access, egress, or vulnerabilities.

- Routine activities of employees, suppliers, customers, and visitors.

- Security protocols or equipment.

- Other relevant information.

Pre-Attack Preparation

During pre-attack preparation, terrorist activities are most vulnerable to detection and can best be halted. Depending on the scope of the attack, preparation may occur over a period of months and, in some cases, years.

Examples of pre-incident preparation activities include:

- Surveillance.

- Security tests.

- Acquisition of supplies and materials.

- Practice or test runs.

Surveillance

Surveillance conducted in preparation for an attack might:

- Take place over several days, weeks, or longer.

- Involve repeated visits to collect needed information about a potential target.

Information Collected Through Surveillance

The following types of information have been collected through adversarial surveillance:

- Locations and numbers of security personnel and cameras

- Facility layout, including access and egress routes

- Timing of routine events

- Event-specific data (relating to special events)

- Security/visitor processes and procedures

- Security equipment, including badges and uniforms

- Information about maintenance and cleaning personnel or procedures

- Crowd data (i.e., when potential targets are the most crowded)

- Access requirements for restricted or employee-only areas

- Parking facility access and operations

Surveillance Activities

Surveillance activities include the following:

- Drawing maps or diagrams

- Observing employees and facilities using vision-enhancing devices (e.g., binoculars, still and video cameras, and night vision goggles)

- Soliciting employees for information

- Taking notes about security and routines

- Charting crowd patterns

- Pocketing documents

- Photographing security equipment, badges, or apparel

- Observing security responses after attempting unauthorized access

Surveillance Activities Can Be Detected

As mentioned earlier in the course, surveillance activities are a weak link in the preparation phase prior to an attack, for the following reasons:

- It takes time. Surveillance may take place over several days, weeks, or longer.

- It may involve repeated visits.

Trained and Untrained Operatives

Surveillance by highly trained individuals can be conducted individually or by teams using a variety of sophisticated surveillance equipment and multiple forms of transportation. Teams may act as families or tourists to gain access to and probe selected targets.

Experience has shown us that individuals involved in planning terrorism are not always well-trained or equipped. Operatives who are not highly trained are more vulnerable to detection by employees, passers-by, and others.

How to Detect Adversarial Surveillance

In order to detect surveillance by adversaries, first you should take note of activities you observe that are typically associated with surveillance, such as watching a location or recording information about it over time.

Next, you should evaluate any surveillance-related activities that you observe to determine if they seem unusual or noteworthy. Often, you will find that surveillance activities will appear unusual and out of place.

Look for Unusual Activities

The key to surveillance detection is knowledge of what is normal for your environment. Review the following examples of normal and unusual activities.

Examples:

Normal Activities	Unusual Activities - Surveillance
A photographer or videographer working on assignment will take photographs openly, use professional equipment, and make efficient use of time.	A person conducting surveillance may try to hide his or her activities, use a cell phone or low-end camera, and make repeated visits.
A tourist usually will take photographs of everything that is notable in the area, and will include companions in them.	An individual conducting surveillance may focus attention on one location, and in particular building entrances, windows, or security personnel or features. If there are companions or others included, they usually are not the focus of a photo or video.

Evaluating Unusual Activities

An unusual surveillance-related activity by itself may not necessarily be an indicator of adversarial surveillance. It is important to assess and evaluate the totality of observed actions and behaviors as well as other relevant circumstances.

For example, a person may be interested in building doors or entrances for a variety of innocent reasons. However, the person's behavior is suspicious and should be reported if the person displays additional unusual behaviors, such as:

- Making repeated visits to the same location to record or document something about the doors or entrances.

- Attempting to disguise an interest in the doors or entrances.

- Displaying more of an interest in alarm and security features or in restricted or employee-only entrances.

Surveillance Scenarios

Instructions: Review each of the following scenarios and identify what is unusual about it.

In each of the following scenarios, an employee or passer-by has observed an unusual activity that could involve adversarial surveillance at that location.

When reviewing the scenario details, take note of any aspects of the situation that seem unusual to you.

Scenario 1: Photography From a Parked Car

Ray is crossing the street toward his workplace in the morning and sees someone taking photos of the building entrance with a camera.

The person taking the photos is sitting inside a car that is parked across the street from the building. The car window is closed and the person is hunched over inside the car.

Question: What is unusual about this person's activities?

Scenario 2: Bus Stop

People gather across the street from Megan's building near a bus stop every day. The bus comes at the same time every hour. People who are waiting check often for an approaching bus and look at their watches or cell phones frequently. They typically wait less than 20 minutes.

One day, Megan notices a man sitting at the bus stop and writing in a notebook. When Megan looks up again almost an hour later, the man is in the same location and does not look up as a bus approaches. Megan sees him several more times in the following week at different times of the day, and he waits for an hour or more each time, writing in his notebook. He looks up often, but only toward her building.

What is unusual about this person's activities?

Scenario 3: Pacing Off Distances

Ella is walking from her car in the employee parking lot. There is a young man in front of her taking long strides. When he reaches the parking lot gate, he stops and writes something in a small notebook.

The young man starts walking again alongside the parking lot fence from one end to the other, stopping again at the end to write in his notebook. When he turns around and sees Ella watching, he quickly puts the notebook in his pocket and rapidly walks away.

Question: What is unusual about this person's activities?

Scenario 4: Going Through the Trash

Marcus is walking behind his workplace when he notices a woman reaching inside a company recycling container. Her attire is much too casual for an employee. There is a stopped car nearby with someone in the driver's seat and the engine running.

The woman pulls out a handful of papers, pages through them, and puts one inside a messenger bag. She sees Marcus, then jams the other papers inside her bag, walks rapidly to the car with her head averted, and gets inside. The car speeds away.

Question: What is unusual about these activities?

Unusual and Suspicious Activities

Other examples of surveillance-related activities that are suspicious if they are conducted in an unusual manner include:

- Taking photographs or videos.

- Using image-enhancing devices such as binoculars.

- Making notes, diagrams, or maps.

- Apparently measuring distances in strides or timing events.

- Watching, visiting, or passing by a location repeatedly over time by the same person or vehicle.

Activities That Always Should Be Reported

Illegal activities always should be reported, following established procedures for your organization and/or local law enforcement guidelines.

In addition, the following activities are always suspicious and should be promptly reported in every instance to a manager or security personnel:

- Questioning employees about security personnel, processes, procedures, and equipment.

- Security tests, attempts to access employee-only or non-public areas, or an increase in alarms or events that require a security or law enforcement response.

- Systems access attempts.

- Thefts or attempted thefts of IDs, badges, or uniforms; smart phones, laptops, or other equipment; or vehicles.

Avoid Aiding and Abetting

The following activities also may be associated with gathering information about a potential target:

- Questioning about building entrances where there may be no security, such as loading docks or the "back door."

- Asking or expecting an employee to hold a door open that requires a key, code, or badge to enter.

You can avoid situations where you might become an unwilling participant in surveillance activities by refusing to answer questions related to building access or allowing an unauthorized person access to restricted areas. If the person persists, inform a manager or security immediately.

Surveillance and Time

As mentioned earlier in this course, surveillance usually involves repeated visits to the location under surveillance. A person engaged in adversarial surveillance may be seen frequently in the vicinity of the object of the surveillance, whether a person or a location.

If you observe the same person repeatedly over time, and that person is engaging in suspicious activities, this could be an indicator that surveillance is taking place.

Surveillance and Location

Persons engaged in surveillance may change location in order to appear less conspicuous and avoid detection. The locations selected typically provide access to information needed for planning an attack or other crime.

You may see the same person conducting surveillance at different locations over a period of time. For example, that person may appear outside the front of your building, inside the building, or in places where you and your coworkers gather, such as a local coffee shop or eatery.

Unusual Behavior

Giveaways of unusual behavior may be as obvious as seeing a person attempting to hide when observed. They also include:

- Reacting visibly to events of interest, such as security guard movements, by moving, communicating, or taking notes.

- Making sudden turns or stops, such as turning around abruptly or ducking into a doorway.

- Making visible hand or other signals to communicate with others on the team.

Behavior: Running and Hiding

In several of the scenarios reviewed earlier in the course, the behavior of the person conducting the surveillance was unusual.

Two mistakes made them more visible to detection and immediately suspect: running and hiding.

- **Running:** The persons immediately and hurriedly fled the area when detected.

- **Hiding:** The persons tried to hide, avert their faces, or duck down or behind something to avoid detection.

Unusual Behavior and Cover Story

Other common mistakes include failing to have a valid reason for being in a particular location or engaging in activities that are not normally conducted in a particular location.

For example, a person may be dressed inappropriately for the environment, such as:

- Wearing overly casual clothing in a professional environment.

- Wearing business or formal attire while claiming to be a maintenance employee.

- Wearing accessories to disguise appearance.

Practice Your Observation Skills

You can identify activities and behaviors that are unusual for your environment through regular observation of what is around you.

Practice your observation skills while entering or leaving your workplace, taking note of people and vehicles that you see, and trying to remember details about them. This will accomplish two purposes:

- You will have a better idea of what is normal for your environment.

- You will become accustomed to recalling information about what you do observe. This will help you to report your observations.

Surveillance Detection Awareness

This narrative illustrates the importance of taking action and reporting surveillance when you observe it.

NARRATOR: Recognizing suspicious behavior and the signs of surveillance are important to protecting our critical infrastructure, key resources, and our American way of life. You are the first line of defense. It is essential to be able to identify, as well as report, potential threats, both in and outside of the workplace. No one knows what looks suspicious in your environment better than you do. There are many scenarios of which you should be aware, including audio/video surveillance, facility access . . .

MAN: Thanks.

NARRATOR: . . . providing access to unfamiliar workers . . .

SECURITY GUARD: Hey!

NARRATOR: . . . ruses and other tricks . . .

[Indistinct conversations]

MAN: There was a security breach at work.

NARRATOR: . . . and cyberattacks. We all play a role in keeping America safe. If you see something unusual, don't hesitate to tell your supervisor, call security, or, in some cases, even the local police. Your safety depends on your vigilance. If you see something, say something.

"If You See Something, Say Something™" used with permission of the NY Metropolitan Transportation Authority.

Reporting

As you go about your daily work, you are in the best position to observe and report unusual activities related to surveillance.

Reporting suspicious activities is invaluable to the work of law enforcement in our shared effort to secure the Nation. Your reporting may be the key to disrupting a planned terrorist or criminal operation.

Organizations can contribute by encouraging employees to report the suspicious activities that they observe.

To Whom Do You Report?

It is a good practice for every place of employment to establish and communicate procedures for reporting suspicious activities to management and law enforcement. These procedures should identify who to contact and when, and include all relevant phone numbers.

If you are an employee, you may need to inform your supervisor, a manager, or security personnel so that they can call your local police. If your company is small, or you work alone, you may be the one who needs to call the local police or other law enforcement contacts.

What Should You Report?

It is a good idea to write down as much information about the person or vehicle you observed and any other information about the incident, in case the police are not immediately able to come out and take a report.

Writing down the details is important—memories only stay fresh for a short time! Include information about the actions or behaviors that you observed as well as descriptions of persons and/or vehicles that were involved.

Your employer or local police department may already have a worksheet available for you to use to record your observations. If not, a sample worksheet is available that you can use.

What Happens to Reports of Suspicious Activity?

The following is a summary of the steps that may be followed to analyze and investigate your report of suspicious activity. Not all steps will be followed for each report—the specific actions taken will be based on the results of analysis or investigation at each step of the process.

1. Individuals - Individuals report suspicious activities

2. Local Security and Law Enforcement - Local security and law enforcement perform initial analysis/investigation

3. NSI Database - Law enforcement organizations enter report into National Suspicious Activity Reporting (SAR) Initiative (NSI) database

4. Intel Centers and Groups - Regional Intelligence Fusion Centers and FBI Field Intelligence Groups analyze NSI Reports

5. Regional and National Law Enforcement - FBI Joint Terrorism Task
    Forces or other law enforcement agencies conduct investigations as
    warranted.

Reporting Observed Activities

In addition to reporting details about the people or vehicles involved, you
should specify in your reporting what about the situation was unusual and
suspicious.

Recall the details of the scenario involving the person at the bus stop and
writing in a notebook over several days. Your report should include your
observations about how the situation is unusual, including

- The person was at the bus stop for longer periods than is normal.

- The person did not appear to be waiting for a bus. For example, the
  person did not look up when a bus approached, nor board one.

- The person appeared to be more interested in the building than the
  bus.

- The person appeared at different times of the day and over several
  days.

Actions To Avoid

Employees who are not trained security or law enforcement officers should
avoid forceful actions when encountering potential surveillance activities.

Examples include:

- Confronting or aggressively questioning suspicious persons.

- Attempting to physically restrain suspicious persons.

- Attempting to confiscate equipment, such as cameras or cell phones.

- Following closely or obviously behind suspicious persons to obtain
  vehicle or other information.

These undertakings may put employees at risk.

Training

To ensure that employees remain vigilant, supervisors and managers should consider:

- Implementing an employee training program.

- Following up the training program by asking questions to assess their understanding of the material.

- Making sure employees remember who to notify if they observe suspicious behavior.

- Regularly reviewing what to report and reporting procedures with employees.

- Encouraging employees to touch base as needed with supervisors and security managers after reporting an incident.

"If You See Something, Say Something™"

The "If You See Something, Say Something™" public awareness campaign video provides a general overview of activities with a possible nexus to terrorism and violent crime and encourages everyone to report these activities to law enforcement.

"If You See Something, Say Something™" used with permission of the NY Metropolitan Transportation Authority.

Community Reporting Initiatives

Many communities across the United States have similar reporting initiatives.

Some of these programs have been in existence for many years and may provide training as well as specific points of contact and reporting mechanisms—such as text or email applications—to report suspicious activities.

Resources

Course Documents

- <u>Surveillance Detection Actions</u>: This is a printable summary of the actions covered in this course.

- <u>Reporting Worksheet</u>: This is a sample worksheet that can be used to record your observations prior to contacting police about suspicious activities.

Training Resources

- <u>Dams Sector Security Awareness Guide: A Guide for Owners and Operators</u> (October 2007)

- <u>If You See Something, Say Something</u>™ (video - 10 minutes): This video was released as part of the Homeland Security campaign to raise public awareness of the indicators of terrorism and violent crime, and to emphasize the importance of reporting suspicious activity.

- <u>Nationwide SAR Initiative Training Web site</u>

- <u>Surveillance Detection Awareness Webisode </u>(video – 1 minute, 22 seconds): This video provides information emphasizing the importance of detecting and reporting suspicious surveillance activities.

- <u>What's in Store: Ordinary People, Extraordinary Events</u> (video - 10 minutes): This video provides information to help employees identify and report suspicious activities and threats in a timely manner.

- <u>Workplace Security Awareness (IS-906)</u>: This online independent study course provides guidance to individuals and organizations on how to improve security in the workplace.

Course Summary

Remember, there are three simple actions that you can take to identify, detect, and report adversarial surveillance activities:

Understand surveillance

- Identify the targets of surveillance.

- Recognize the purpose of surveillance.

- Know what information is collected during surveillance.

Detect Surveillance

- Look for unusual behavior or activities.

- Recognize the indicators of adversarial surveillance.

Report surveillance

- Determine (in advance) procedures for reporting incidents:

    o   Within your organization.

    o   To local law enforcement.

- Report suspicious activities using predetermined procedures and forms.